ALONE WITH EVERYONE

THE UNCOLLECTED POEMS

BENJAMIN SALTMAN

SAN LUIS OBISPO, CALIFORNIA

ALONE WITH EVERYONE

THE UNCOLLECTED POEMS

BENJAMIN SALTMAN

Some of these poems have previously appeared in the following magazines and periodicals to whose editors grateful acknowledgment is made: *Epoch, Slant, Poetry Northwest, Aethlon: The Journal of Sport Literature, Beyond Baroque Magazine, Shirim, Bakunin, Poetry/LA, Crosscurrents, Asylum, Santa Monica Review,* and *The Hudson Review.*

Alone With Everyone. Copyright © 2018 by Ben and Helen Saltman and Phoenix Press. All rights reserved. Printed in the United States of America. No part of this book may be reproduced in any manner whatsoever except in the case of brief quotations embodied in critical articles and reviews or without written permission of the author.

Editor: Nicholas Campbell

Cover art and design by Nicholas Campbell and Helen Saltman. A special thanks to Helen Saltman and Michael Sheen Campbell for proofreading this book. Thanks also goes out to poet Jason Wooi-Chin.

For information address the Phoenix Press at 5969 Entrada Avenue, # 9, Atascadero, CA 93422 or call 805-461-0579.

Special thanks to W.S. Merwin for the blurb on the back cover. Photograph of Benjamin Saltman on page 129 by Helen Saltman © 1993 and 2017. Photograph of Bert Meyers on page 119 by Elliot Erwitt © 1968 by Doubleday & Company, Inc.

ISBN-13: 978-1986602297 ISBN-10: 198660229X

For those I love. You know who you are.

TABLE OF CONTENTS

A Room in a Small Town/13-14

Dragonfly/15

Mirror for Daughters/16

A Game of Marbles/17-18

Little Stories/19

The Candle/20

Rilke's Black Cat/21

The Winter Pruning/22

In the Valley Everything is What It Seems/23

The Curves of Bridges/24

As You Sit in Darkness/25

How I Got Here/26

The Visit/27-28

Mornings around Six/29-30-31

The Rain Flies Up/32

A Sort of Fame /33

Rain in America/34-35

Pittsburgh to the Bone/36

Adding Things Up/37

The Plaza at the Museum of Contemporary Art/38

Afternoon Movie/39

The Swimming Bee/40-41

Words, Again/42

Garibaldi in Lombardy/43

Moishe/44

Father and Son/45

To Die by Datsun, to Live by Pralines and Cream/46-47

Smoking Camels Passively/48

My People/49

The Grass Where the Dead Walk Quietly/50-51

Winters and Winters/52-53

The Miscarriage/54

Grape Vine, I Will Not Let You Go/55

Always the Falls/56

Take Me Out of the Sun/57-58

Burning the News/59

Homage to My City/58-59

Jewish/60

A Treatise on Work/61

At Home in the Underpass/62

The News in Translation/63-64

The Greenhouse Effect Reaches the Environmental Agency/65

The Quake/66-67

Old Mrs. Gilbert's House at Fox Hollow/68

For K./69

Arbor/70-71

The Hawk/72

Because You Took Three Spoons of Sugar/73

My Hopi Buckle/74

Spacing/75-76

The Utility Man/77

He Has Won a Prize/78

Judgement/79-80

Acquitting the Looters/81

My Fate: Unocal/82

Fractals/83

Dogs Welcome/84-85

The Phone Rings/86-87

Barney Ross/88-103

Other Writings/105

To Those Who Would Read Me/107-111

Letter from Benjamin Saltman, 1993/113-115

An Alaskan Special/117-118

Coughing With Bert/119-128

Biographical Note/129-130

Praise Page/131-132

Excerpt from a letter from Benjamin Saltman to Nicholas Campbell, dated April 3, 1992:

Dear Nick.

I have cleared up my business with the Office of Research and Sponsored Projects; I owed them a report on the money they gave me last summer to put together *Alone with Everyone*.

Your friend,

Ben

Equipped with his knowledge of human psychology and physiology, the Acmeist was to 'adjust' —not in gloomy resignation but joyfully— to reality, and in the strictness of self-imposed forms write balanced, clear poems about it all.
—Clarence Brown

Who knows, at the mention of 'farewell,'
What separation awaits us,
What the cockscrow augurs
When flames glow on the acropolis,
And in the dawn of some new life
While an ox chews lazily in his shed,
Why the cock, herald of new life,
Beats his wings on the town's walls?
—Osip Mandelstam

A ROOM IN A SMALL TOWN

Something is everywhere.
You look for it
at the furthest end
of the smallest capillary
where the blood can no longer go.
And in that space is something.

When you arrive you open your eyes.
You set up your room and hot plate
and put your humble socks in the drawer
so you can have long conversations
about some things.

Since everyone is there
you don't need to think of
good and bad or hot and cold,
you know you invited everyone
even though it sickens you,
even though it elates you.
You have always wanted to be
alone with everyone.

It is a great relief
like finding the first blade of grass
on a strange planet.
Since this is everything
all your acts arrive
empty as a cool veranda
after the day's heat.
There are groups,
networks, there is joy
in the body's night
gritty with stars.

You have violated privacy

and feel for a moment
the iron hand
of your secret life,
but you are recognized by wallpaper,
by the sink curving its arms,
by the window caressing your cheek.
They know you.
Something is here.

DRAGONFLY

I see myself with pale wings, two pair,
no, Handiwrap wings, iridescent,
blue twig body, toothpick body hanging
over the nasturtiums, hungry for gold,
for bugs, for what lives in gardens
as I fire and hang, fire and hang.
And my head like a club.

The light outside the mind
catches me in ignorance,
why I land and why I go;
because what thinks me has made me
as I blur between heavy leaves;
thought dissolves, and I falter.

What has made me can't know me.
I see myself erode in someone's mind,
fade away and flare out again;
and suddenly my body is a velvet pin,
I am a retinal smear, I build a nest
in a bend of twigs, or under eaves,
or on a hill of grass, anywhere.
I am desperate to be.

This morning, when the sun
picks out a spider strand,
I fire my arrow at a fold of brain,
I slide along a thin sheet of air,
my blue pen is always writing.

MIRROR FOR DAUGHTERS

I am where my daughters are, their eyes
turn me into theirs; yet I have aged so far
I must look hard to find myself in them
as if in the window or car door.

As for me, I used to laugh
to keep the darkness down. Was I so eager
to be knowing everything? And so wakeful?
Across the room they slip outside my mind
where I won't be going.
They have me wondering what I'll lose.

They will wait for me a little longer,
I suppose.

A GAME OF MARBLES

In those days he always won,
and lost only to his mother.
She would take him by his arm
and drag him back to the Old Country.
He took the green glass
from his pocket, held it on his palm,
smoke curled at its center.

It was a great day to win,
it was American to win.
On his knees in the dirt strip
between the curb and fence, he felt
his shoulder blades take flight
into the All-American heart of the city.
Howard laughed, Josey
was afraid to play. "You got
your good ones." "How much you win
last time?" And the air reached
and folded hands around him.

The air was kind and did not tell
that his mother talked Jewish.
And the marbles, the chipped ones,
the smooth and gritty ones
in the red net bag on the dirt
lay quietly in sexual ease.
(In his house, he knew, his mother
brandished tea and cigarettes
over her bitter losses).
And the etched circle in hard dirt
held four marbles, agates, light glitter,
a big glass grape, these drops
of his desire to disappear
and leave his Jewish face behind.
His shot skidded, hit, clinked, clean,

spurted across the ground
as a blessing of sudden flight, and
stuck in the middle of American earth,
his promised land. And looking
down at the glass ball's creamy swirl,
he saw that he could win them all,
drive each marble skittering
across the line into his possession
forever. Behind him the houses
lined up their bricks as he knuckled
in the dirt, fired his thumb
against his crooked forefinger,
and launched into the world.

LITTLE STORIES

The shadow of the roof
cuts across the orange tree
with the thought that you might leave me.
    I understand such emotions.
But because nothing ever happens
in the future
             I wonder what
goes on in this house, this yard.
It must be informal,
it has always hidden itself
    beneath surprising repetitions.

It doesn't matter what I want to do,
I am the place where myths enact themselves,
the essential ones,
                the myth of paper,
of peach, of shoe. At times I almost
feel the presence of such kind stories
    without knowing them.

They put a fine edge on your face
and hands and on the rooftops
floating over an evening walk,
                sustaining hope
in breath and gravity
on which we casually live.

These tales combine to form
                the table of forgetting
and the oak chair, desire,
where we may sit and talk
    and where your face exists.

THE CANDLE

I looked into the blue heart
and touched transparent wax
in the cup below the candle flame. The pool
hugged my finger as the flame shuddered,
and put a white hat on my fingerpad.
I was mitred like a priest. I hope
that whatever hurts is mixed with light.
Then the silken wax I rolled
into a ball dropped back into the flame,
and the wax slipped into itself
quickly, as if ordered by the light.
The light went on correcting the little
smooth-lipped bowl it drank from
gazing at the plume of fire.
I counted seconds I could keep
my finger in the flame, I held my palm
hovering over the tip of pain.
I could see the black wick and center of fire,
so went on looking as the hissing blue
floated far back in my eyes, cool.

RILKE'S BLACK CAT

As usual the man got lost in what he saw.
First the black sank into him, into his pores,
became the dark sheen
of tiny wells within his skin,

and turned his arrogant face
toward sensuality.
He could have called it terror,
necessary to his way of knowledge.

Then it loomed up like a huge cloud
in the future of German darkness.
And between the midnight and himself
there grew a paw.

So he was gone. He had the politics
and absorbency of a sleepy animal.
Merely waiting, he could make a world,
imagination was a form of thought;

yet his "Schwarze Katze" became so physical
it was a dream in which ideas collapsed.
It was a trick as well, cat and poem,
in which all space could find itself.

And of each word of fear he made an angel.
And to each angel he gave amber eyes.

THE WINTER PRUNING
Morris and Clara

The white cut wood stumps all over the tree
looking for sympathy. I am guilty for everything
cut off, I violated the Thou Shalt Not Prune
commandment. Not allowed to turn away or whimper I
was the gardener of all the deaths,
I carry a pruning pole like a guillotine.
It's up to me to create forgetting.
Sometimes loss dreams gardens,
and a flowering apricot dripping petals.
Loss puts in place what will come after,
but I have a long vigil while the white stumps
gradually darken, pinched closer every season.

With leaves, the whisper of the tree embeds in air,
but do I kill all those twigs for their own good?
The tree goes headlong into mourning its bitter resin,
but the new branches are ways to forget, I
have to brush them back to find the puckered wood.
The new year's apricots will ripen into pink balls
of new babies. The space my mother and father
would have occupied belongs to others,
stuttering with pollen, bearing other names.

IN THE VALLEY EVERYTHING IS WHAT IT SEEMS

The wasp-nest mother curls over the bullet cells,
and the young apricots have begun their trembling
in early April. Another final middle-class spring.
Everybody rubbing feelers all over each other
in a hectic business like the commodities
exchange as if there were no center to these
greetings. The rush to a millennium is now at full
skimming hummingbird speed. Can't I see?
Must I always swim in forgetfulness? The bottle-
brush buds are strung along their stems frozen
like rap singers waiting for the music.

This is the end. The theorists have peeled themselves
and left no residue. Dust-motes and gnats
purl in the sucking sun. It is time
to take down the curtains and wash them
in the growling machine, then to walk the yard
holding a cordless phone. With nothing else to do,
the flowers cry out for recognition. It is time
to join them as they furl and unfurl,
and to stop counting, just stop counting.

THE CURVES OF BRIDGES

Sometimes a bridge makes me leap out
like the best ball I threw when I was twelve
heading for home from center field
leaping from one island to another
with a fine arc and hanging from cables of air.
Just to be there tells me I want to go
where they point gray fingers at Yerba Buena Island
red fingers at Marin. Few things will go
over bridges normally, light things like pollen
or a cat's greeting. A bridge stretches its rails
and grins and takes off terribly at night,
a runway under the thunder of wings, escapes
from everything that was—the condemnations
and even the good trees on the near side
wringing their leaves. There is always
the courage, even the weary courage of a crowded
day captured in a car radio hammered.
I am always on a bridge when I realize how far
the water is below, flung and swept and spittled.
A bridge like a long bird flying trailing its legs.
And when bridges fall we sit up in bed and stare.

AS YOU SIT IN DARKNESS

You can almost believe
that a fingernail contains
its whole history.
But you can't believe it.

Everything can be lost.
What you remember becomes
why you remember.
And you wonder why.

The air changes
and the leaves begin to sizzle
like bacon.
Reconciliation

requires an opening so wide
it looks up softly
with the blue gaze
of a baby.

HOW I GOT HERE

Where have I been? The silence in each
brick has been fashioned by the years

I love those endless places
and want justice for the dead minutes

But their names have been taken away
and the directions have curled and fallen

Each act I have done hoping to change
hoping to keep the same leads to a moment

when I cry for help, when I say
look I'm here. What have you done

to make so much inevitable? Let me
have their names so I can thank them

and ask for friendship and open
up into time like a swimmer feeling

for life everywhere. The future can't be
as amazing as these trees and faces

that move and fade and then appear
while I dive and dream in unknown water

THE VISIT

When I saw you again
and your wife smiling
I knew that
the gully you showed us
with the red berries
rigid and trembling
was waiting ready to burn,
and I would have offered
my friendship again
and we might hope for renewal
but there was nothing important
to talk about.
Your idea about others
was that they should listen.

We had wanted to change
and had changed
shaking hands warmly
for twenty years,
and with the binoculars
you handed me I saw
the grey kestrel
at the top of the tree
as if it were your kestrel.
It was waiting to rise
then fall on something small.

Once we thought that somehow
a gift would come upon us,
some reward.
I couldn't ask you
whether it had come,
you might have said it had,
said with glazed eyes what I
would hear in pain.

I saw how we walked quietly
on Hall Canyon Road
into our next life
and the road
disappeared behind us
as if satisfied
that it had taken us this far.

MORNINGS AROUND SIX

1.

What happens has already
happened when it occurs
to you, you already see
yourself falling in the past.
The hard part is acceptance
while you fall, even as a pang of loss
takes you by the throat.
Oh, and you think of what
will be broken in the future,
the time you fractured your wrist
and the pebbles stippling
the heel of your right hand.
You see the past as a fall
into the future, you hunch your shoulders
thinking, Let it come,
I love this life.

The hard part is to know that
either to resist or not
is the right thing to do,
that to fight not even knowing
whether to fight is worthwhile.
It is of you to admit these things,
and to give up pretending not to know.
In any case you will fall.
You have seen the leaves resist,
twirl and resist until the last
few brown veins remain
to fall strangely, too late, in midsummer.
The hard part is to be a leaf
and to know it, to cling by your mouth
as you swing and tear
across a few months, jerked by rain.

You know how to be a leaf
or anything else, you must know,
and that is the hard part.

2.

Giving up the summers is hard,
past summers smelling of gasoline,
when your father made no money.
The weather was billowy,
your lungs filled like balloons,
and you moved on your toes
quick with counterpunches.
How much more could you give up
from the beginning as an early offering?
Who will you be when you
surrender the fear and memory
of the steaming summers, the chill nights?
You might give up, for example,
the lace-up boots with the jackknife pocket.
Or your father holding his failures by the wrist.

Those times, those times and that God.
The snails, the answering files,
the damp bed at night—
they stick to you, emotion soaked.
If you were to obliterate them
simply, without preamble,
they would never leave you.
Your emptiness would be
the measure of their presence.
At that time what you were
and what you did was shadowed:
it was of your making.
You know now that it was not just memory,
that snail of all snails,
no different from you,

it could never be simply abandoned.
You would become the snail,
and any separation or difference
would remain an illusion.
Yet you were always other than memory.
You never stopped creating what you are,
even the land, palpable, with a bloody lip,
the sour taste of feathers.
Giving up those summers is hard.
See how they hold on until you bless them.

THE RAIN FLIES UP

All night it spilled onto the brick patio
its secret of having no will and nothing to oppose.
The cats were staring at the windows
as if what they saw would make them fabricate a life
connected to a great vein in the earth.

Rain embraces the worm loose as cellophane,
rain is the persistent wedding of puddles.
It wants to bring us together, and politicians rush
from trembling cars bowing.
Stolid downtown buildings blur.

The last words of rain are skeined by filtration plants,
but the rain isn't there, it waits curved
in a water glass, its meniscus imitates the moon.
It brings down cargoes of small life,
lifting and dropping the ancient world. Thus

the future is with children or sheep or nothing,
we'll walk into the future like falling and rising water,
drop by drop running together, sinking in fields,
sucked up in trees, to open our eyes in leaves,
never passing a grain of sand without a touch,
to shine and shiver since nothing is over.

A SORT OF FAME

When you enter the tanned heart of the white wood
of violated furniture in the best stores
long after the bark has been torn away,
you may feel that the path of the grain
will lead you from table to panel
into comfortable public sleep
at the May Company or Ethan Allen
in soft country smelling of wax.
You enter a hush of anesthetized bedrooms. The journey
goes through clear pine, teak, velvet walnut, oak, then
into water dreams, codes
faint and delicate as consciousness;
oily water, swirls, the look of drowned peacock feathers,
the woodgrain in the land of Oak Barn! Of Antique Guild!

And some of us are split like that, polished and sealed,
soaked with strain, polyurethaned, displayed.
It happens. In our voices you can barely hear
the knock of axes. The grinding leaves.
An old glassed dining room table,
oval, dark as chocolate, reflects the memory of Mother
raising a cup of tea to false teeth. So does wood promise us
if we apply ourselves. We shall take part in the grain, rest
in exposed gleaming versions of having lived.
Such promises whirl at our fingertips.

RAIN IN AMERICA

1.
It shines the used car lots, the light multiplies.

2.
They can't find each other
in the same room unless the chairs move.

Over the biggest cities above the clouds
the stars swing their chains.
There are purple bruises, and the courts
are full of claimants.

3.
Sirens and lights.
The wet machines will not let them die,
they force them to be born.

4.
A helicopter tumbles into the river
which rubs its brown hands across the splinters.
America is all news.

5.
The candidates can't see themselves yet, destruction
washes them in its yellow light. People
fall into car seats and face the road,
embarrassed because they must learn the art of poverty.
Mist, pebbled windows, the end of an age.

6.
Someone stands waving like an insect
from the top of a sunken house.

7.
The candidate says, "We will not throw away

our great gifts." The people demonstrate now
in front of the kind guns.

PITTSBURGH TO THE BONE

My mother soaked the stones.
The house pressed my forehead
and rushed elongated leopards between tombstones,
long spotted clouds at streetlight level.
Soot drifted down my cheek
until my heart leaped even at black leaves.
At night the flashes
sodden red at the roofline pulsed
when the Bessemer Converters opened bottles
and my father's soul rushed out
peddling old-fashioned dresses to the sky.

After fifty years of change
milkweed grows in sandy patches.
Each corner indents a mini-mall,
I've been to every franchise everywhere.
When I drive past tall blue four-by-fours
I know building still goes on,
falling still goes on—
dusty saws are soaked in power.
A fine breeze from tv's
plays from skeleton condos.
Pepsi machines cough in cages.
The soot is gone
but I long for the deep breath
that filled my lungs with the ache of gasoline.

ADDING THINGS UP

I write calmly of the room
with the rust-colored carpet,
I am not different
even though my skin tells me
otherwise. What hears me
across the distances
has been talking to me, we
have been meeting like this.

There is a small potted tree
in my living room and a leaf
presses against the cheap curtain,
and the sun imprints a lace shadow
on the leaf. Meanwhile the pattern
has moved onto the wood floor.
I wonder if I can confess
that this is all I will ever have.

THE PLAZA AT THE LA MUSEUM OF CONTEMPORARY ART

I'm from nowhere.
When I walk here the new city
lifts its shoulders inside the old,
glass collects the faces.
This city is too big for people.

Angles and colors stroll around the fountain.
Over in a corner
the police are beating Rodney King.
Amid this merciless art
people sit on stone benches for lunch
with plastic wrap and cold coffee.
They shimmer.

The faces are so different
they are the same. The word for them
is one, the sound is one,
unlike mine. They are one and I am many,
the museum is full of me
shuffling and creaking.

AFTERNOON MOVIE

After the credits rolled
people stood in the light confused,
they began to slide along the rows
and you said, "Where for desert?"

After the pie I was in the yard,
things were still in a Saturday aura
like the dazzle I've seen with wet eyes
swimming in sunlight.
I grew up on movies.

It wasn't a good movie but that didn't matter.
In its haze nothing else was real.
A few leaves fell from the apricot
and the webs and dusty glass inside the toolshed door
wore a glove of shadows.

Yellow and black moths were crawling
over the flowering mint, too bright and clear,
and I couldn't believe any of it.
It was all clear and I couldn't believe it.
"It's no good to combine a movie and sunlight,"
I said. "Why should it be good?" you said.

And yet we had gone to the movie
for a part of us to be set aside,
believing we could return.
Huge faces we had left back in the Cineplex
appeared in the trees,
and the hats of houses over the wall
imitated roofs we wanted to be there.
I didn't want to be there.

THE SWIMMING BEE

Like dead bees I'd seen in the pool before,
this bee was done, nothing moved
unmoved by the water.
I saw him limp on the swells
next to my nose,
and when I pulled back
he slipped into the trough with ease.

My touch was almost accidental,
a nudge goodbye.
But then he moved in little kicks.
Not drowned? He was a tiny ball
of wet yarn with legs like hair.
I treaded water
bathed in green by the dwarf orange
leaning over me.
I picked him by a wing from the water
and set him on dry concrete
to let the sun he'd gathered
bathe him for the last time.

But he began a crippled crawl.
Undead, he began to haul his plumpness
over the hot walk, like baggage
on a despairing trip to the last train.
Whether he was full or empty of pollen
when he fell in the water
I couldn't tell.
I thought his job was done anyway.

Then he stopped on the burning stone.
Lank filament wings fanned and blurred
once, twice, and he began to scrub
his head pulling and unfurling
his thin trunk. Then, shimmying,

he washed his back with air.
For ten minutes he stumbled in a circle,
his legs went everywhere. For ten minutes
more I watched him dry himself fuzzy.

Saw his sudden leap, angle off, zip.
I slipped down in the water,
almost embarrassed,
buried my hot arm in the cool water.

WORDS, AGAIN

It was your faith that you could return
to the honeyed land seen through amber.
There leaves would suddenly spring into being
and you could carefully set down the three blessings,
tin scraping, egg-yolk hardening, butter . . .

Nothing lured you into speech
in the moment of your arrival, your throat
was locked, your heart was in your throat.
You stretched out like a horizon, and the light,
like blood, began to flow.

But you knew that you could not stay,
the cold had entered with your clothes,
with your scratched books and letters.
You called on forests, on Athena,
and the slight tremor in your hands

silently, because with your first words
you would be forced to leave again.
You considered what those inevitable words
might be, how they would catch the bitterness
of the soft light on the window ledge

and lead you, shaken, among others again.
Meanwhile you waited, breathing slowly
the absolutely temporary air, then
under your breath, not to be heard,
recited the names of poet after poet.

GARIBALDI IN LOMBARDY

It was good to change the world.
"By seven o'clock that evening they breasted
a hill and through the trees saw below them
Lake Maggiore shimmering like a trout on grass."
The magnetic murmur of the people
congealed into a new leader.
Castelletto was quiet
for passage of the army of the future
along the street, a lion's shadow,
energy that painted the walls moon-white.

He was teaching his soldiers the strange dance
of the next century. How you skip when hit by
swift technology.
Heavy feet and red scarves, and the air
tasting faintly of dust.
The water did not change
in the stone fountain in the square.
The pearly lice eggs glued to the hair
of confused soldiers testified to the fidelity of nature
and to the future. Every homeland in the grip
of a false father,
a man on a horse with a chest of satellites
and guerillas. The hooves, the jingling,
the muffled laughter made up
the new language of pain.

MOISHE
    A photo, 1942

In a desert of snow we see the black
insect backs of the dead,
they drag sleds loaded with children
who don't know how to look afraid in wool caps.
The ice-shagged mittens hang.
The shawls of smoke whisper about the cold.
"Don't mind us, we think we're going to die,
but first we leave our homes."
They drown in winter.

Indelible black and white,
memory of an old birth wound, they left behind
the dark villages. And the one in front,
the one with a star
trudges under pliable transparent skin
out of the picture,
gassed, tossed, burned, received
at the edge of the town
like a murderer to break our screens.

We ask history to surprise us.
But the moon goes on shaving his head, knocking him down,
fire goes on talking to him.
He arrives under the lights in a parking lot
next to a car in our year,
our sharp breath.

FATHER AND SON

On the picnic in Highland Park
near the granite symbol of Progress
he threw grass on his father and mother
as if to bless them,
to scatter shreds of grass
to damn them.
Old enough at six to know
he had to go.
The secret grass under the blanket,
when the blanket moved, was crushed and warm.
In the steel thermos cup the lemonade
swam with silver.
There! Grass in the lemonade
and the moon rolled up, it was his book.
He would remember his mother
and the twilight down the grass slope
which was his father.

He saw himself glide
in the vague steel haze of parked cars his future
when his steer-eyed father
loomed after him, breaking
out of Russia, trying to get
among the cars and free.

TO DIE BY DATSON, TO LIVE BY PRALINES AND CREAM

We passed the wreck's sullen sparkle, the torn rims,
looking for bodies,
the late July quiet, hands numb.
The evening sky that waited for the ambulance
was blue as the hollow eyes of God
above the slumped Datsun.
Who was hurt or dead?
I looked for someone who could be crying out.

Off the freeway in a blast of light
that washed the trees white
floated an ice cream store, glass and posters,
a boy in a blue shirt, a man in an apron leaning
at a machine. They were down the embankment
and were concerned with summer
while our light was pink,
pink flares, dark faces. A cop stood with a pencil
counting everybody, everything. If
we had all seen each other there we might have
exchanged a moment's envy.
He knew what to count, it seemed,
and we were comfortable.
A corpse with a cracked head at a window
ate pralines and cream in a sugar cone.
White light, rubber lids, cold steam rising
from the ice cream tubs stretched out dead
on the concrete and reflectors.

In our procession the tail lights dripped red
as we stopped and went and stopped.
A match struck in our faces
would have shown the eyes we wouldn't show each other.
The ice cream man sat in the Datsun nodding,

then the ambulance van
smooth as a dolphin nudged into,
as we stared back, those still living.

SMOKING CAMELS PASSIVELY

Down the beach the black girl in the white bikini
and the white girl in the black bikini
are smoking, and the flawed air carried
by an angel of breezes brushes me.
It seems that all my life
I have breathed this lightness and darkness.
Smoking second-hand for twenty years
in stale restaurants, beer bleachers,
I drew community into my veins.
Smoke became my cloudy fingernails. I was
the smoke that passed across my skin,
soaked my shirt, curled around the hair
of my forearms. I walked through
a thousand doors of smoke.
It was the suntan of my teeth.

All that time I drank poison, ate poison,
floated on my back in poison. My evenings glowed
like cigarettes sinking below the horizon.
Now I draw in deeply, when it passes,
a charged, delirious smoke
mixed with the exhausted smell of burning sand,
the aching breath of the girls walking.

MY PEOPLE

They scratch themselves with penknives
on arms and faces and can never do the work
that makes them human.
Their commerce is scattered on dark soil.

  At the corner of Bryant and Belmar
or along the Sahara of Parthenia Street
where windy nights and glint of chrome
occupy the backs, money and capsized, of hands,
they push market carts full of snow and cry out
in Russian, showing their tattooed tongues:
   I listen.
I hear hopelessness like a dog's
who trots panting down the street.

And when I think they will not be helped,
that sugar of light will dissolve before it reaches them,
I realize I'm one of them, made of acid and cloth,
and have never been any other.

GRASS WHERE THE DEAD WALK QUIETLY

That other day—where the dead walk quietly
their eyes yellow roses
the institution wavers, the aggregate walls
waver and fields of short grass
resolve until they grow gigantic
loom in consciousness/ become huge walls
of consciousness
                       all to heaven
green and alive for light feet of spirits

the dead blades intermixed with the living
praying, calling roots to order

clipping that dread feather warm breath.

Pervasive/ tufts in the ears of rocks
crab and devil scuttling the lawns
fiefdoms, strongholds

. . . . .

Undeniable grass in leas in lush spring
fountaining, lifting and bowing modestly
more universal than particular.

Among the headstones the Beloved Parent
less than particular/ the flowers in glass brick
memory grown stupid
hassocks trailing hurt moronic hair over streams.

Grass arrives for the dull meditations of victims
who will eat tastelessly forever. Green/ blue-green/
gripping the pale brain

The lap for babies, the disposable/

the sweet rot steaming, stain, the unforeseen
grass the dew blanket lifted on prongs of stars.

WINTERS AND WINTERS

1.
We promised to construct the past again
we all contributed to the photographs of the dead/
which made them whole
and of corpse-carriers
standing deep in cold mud in wrappings
baring their teeth.

The children were set free from life
their skins cracked and opened
and the roads reflected the passing iron in puddles/
in gleam and smell of chemicals
everything was gathered: the wirephotos

the bits of fingernail/ the hotdog color of the bodies
wrapped carefully the knots tied over the names/
all saved from pure loss
the rattle indistinguishable
from what happened back there.

2.
Even winter wants to live
to count tomorrows in snow bursts
                                        Ah, leave the kitchen/
there are blue eyes in the silence.
Go up to the mountain, there's no smell of oil
your ambition to be water grows/
when you keep moving
and marble glimmers on the branches
there's no end to the year.

Look through the small door
stretch/
you love the death that leaps to your chest
like a youngest daughter.

THE MISCARRIAGE

1.
I fire a gun into the ground

2.
There is a fiat behind my heart/
I can't lean back in my chair

3.
I climb a tree and the fruit bursts

4.
I walk in and out of rooms carrying blood

5.
Someone throws a dollar of flesh into the river,
it skips three times

6.
"Grow up!" I cry at a small boy
riding my shoulders pinching my ears,
he won't let me mow the lawn

7.
A woman crawls on hands and knees
around the world/ she's singing.
I greet her merrily and we buy a farm

GRAPE VINE, I WILL NOT LET YOU GO

You cluster of Argus eyes,
pearlette, smug, ankle bracelet,
leaves like a trail of girls
with wide dresses, fingers
with intimate fuzz.
Your thin arm hangs down reaching
for a friendly wooden hand.
You radiant green for spiders
to hang out their playing fields,
your books go on dragging
the slipping air.
Every escarpment of leaves
reminds the yard of your unripeness,
and faith. Of sawing. Of stairs.
Of work and waiting.
If you don't find anything
you're looking for, you'll find me.
What if the birds get you? Then autumn?
One of your leaves holds
four holes for death to look through.
But I will keep you for my spine
and for your green.
You nod upside down in the wind,
you consume posts and windows,
concrete, barbecue, and, sucking hard
through a tattered ancient stalk,
milky secrets underground.

ALWAYS THE FALLS
                Big Sur, 1989

Of course they aren't the same,
and I can't find the burned tree
that meant something then, and there
created me, at least the part that saw it.
The redwoods balance merely on their crooked hands
as they did, but differently, some catastrophe
smells inside the wood. Helen says the paths
are even more worn, she can't come here again.

But no one ever did, I had no idea
how many of me there were, like leaves,
like the mud. The lord I named then
has done for me many times since then.
The falls have always failed to lie down,
they stand high above the stream.

Since then I've become a colony, each member
negotiates its territory and cries out for justice.
Whose justice? Who is the attorney?
We gather together like a troop of little men
fighting among each other, until we reach the falls
and look up. There is no compromise
the way the water bursts from high in a tree,
then slides down the rock bathing moss and lichen
on the way as if everything were constant.
As if there is no end, and nothing said about returning,
in any state.

TAKE ME OUT OF THE SUN
               —Sampson Naval Hospital, 1946

Down the shining floor of the TB ward
the beds ranged their white staples.
And pinned in each bed a coughing man
shuddered; each remembered his night sweats.
No sympathy for these sailors
intruded on the bacilli doing nature's work.
In them the second world war continued
given to the corpsmen to practice
with pills and needles in their fading bodies.
The needle plunges, the body twitches
like a mouse in a meadow in the shadow of wings
and talons.

        Now all are dead, or sit with white
eyebrows observing television. The hospital
has disappeared in weeds and tough brush
in a corner of New York State,
hardly available to national memory.
Language can't retrieve those rasping throats.
Not even the daybooks mean what they said,
that so many thousands came, so many died
and glided out at night on gurneys
pushed by hushed attendants.

            In the breeze-blown
hissing afternoon the white death is nothing,
and these men huddled over lesions, little flames
trembling in their lungs, are nothing. What is forgotten
remains in the meadow: hallucinations wave,
heat rises, wrapped in newspaper, broken glass,
the old meadow crossed by moths and wasps,
corpsmen and needles, and a dying man
who was a sailor and is not even bone,
is crying in his fever, "Take me out of the sun!"

BURNING THE NEWS

In the fireplace the paper lies
shuddering under kindling wood.
Yesterday's *Times* lies in the heat
with words crawling on its face.
Words about the quake are quaking
those about the riot are running,
those about the fire become
a brown bubble bursting.
People I knew were hurt, their glass
was broken, they lost their usual acts.

My wrists remember the ritual unfoldings
of the headlines, how the paper's wings opened
and we were lost again in China.
Yesterday the fireplace was cold
waiting for the impossible news,
the logs were heavy. Now
the kindling burns
and tails of flame return the page
to its first heat, and push
my hand away. This act of forgetting
demands an axe, matches, and cool weather.

The process of fire:
the valley of paper returns to
the mountains and floats among dead trees;
the fire takes the sad stories back
to where they were molecular.
People rise up like lace petals,
ashes torn into the air, wings only,
bodiless, they fly up and disappear.
Ashes are the wings of catastrophes,
like last breath that hisses at first,
then whisps to nothing in cold air.

HOMAGE TO MY CITY

There are three items to the bag.

On the bus you noted the stiffness of the people.

Since the waitress was tired, she tried to sit down between customers. No soap.

Exigencies. Melancholy. Vocabulary.

Mike Tyson will give an interview
on Wednesday.

An elaborate hospital is going up.

The 7-Eleven on the boundary between city and county does a good business.

Negotiations are proceeding. Abortion is still
a hot topic.

When it rains, close the window. The police
can detain you.

Fragrance.
The magazine, rifled, lies on the bathroom counter.

How many times have you opened that package?

I think the word interactive
really helps.
Party makeup, then ice cubes.

Have you gone there often? It depends
on what level.
There's a shoe store.

Conrad Giesen of the Pico district.

I've gone there often.
If you want to know, the cars throw off a lot of heat.

Mi casa es su casa.

A lot of times.

JEWISH

The Protocols of Zion are wrong;
we will not take over the world,
we have already taken the world.
For ages we have made blood sacrifices
so that we will all finish together.
The Sabbath of all people,
the bread and wine of all people.
We are what you imagine, and you imagine
yourselves. We have been afflicted
by ten plagues; we refuse to go free.
When I walk my street
with my singing dog,
and we pass beneath the fir tree
full of Jewish squirrels eating pine nuts,
I know that we are brothers and sisters,
we help children, we prepare the feast.

A TREATISE ON WORK

All work is useless.
Today cleaning the alley is spiritual discipline,
useless. I watch the ants run to safety.
It must be a responsible thing
to make way for the Fire Department
in case the yard starts burning,
and to force a path for the man from Water and Power
so he can read the meters.

The cement block wall throws down heat,
the leaves pointing from the bottle brush
shake the light at me, and sweat
is kissing and stinging my eyes.
Sometimes I think I have
all the power and light I need.

The sun is ticking at my ear
and I still wonder why I'm doing this
as I wrestle dusty two-by-fours
and a coiled cable I've never known
what to do with. Yet if
each thing is a shell,
the rusted Danish cookie can
holds myself, the bent wire frames
for tomato plants we haven't planted
hold out spiked ends to press down
this summer into the ground of being.
And the path I make parallels the house and wall
like pure intention.

AT HOME IN THE UNDERPASS

There are dark jewels in the tunnel
under the freeway at Mayall,
broken glass glitters
from the streetlight down the road,
my mother, my father, my sister
lying in the glass.
the quilt that is evil, that is fear,
takes me by the arms when I walk here.
Tunnels remind me of tunnels—
not everything can be as simple as bread,
as a philosopher's table.

Sometimes with an armful of groceries from Vons
I think I will drop everything and run
if someone shouts.
So far no one; but that doesn't matter,
expectation matters
and the mind in labor.

The flutter of the traffic overhead
is the swish of blood I hear from my pillow.
The hollow grating sound of my steps
is the sound of my relationships.
I'd prefer to live in a place less real,
less damaging to my shoes, my morale,
with fewer smells, with more hope.
Yet when I walk here in daylight
I look down at the ambiguous water
and up at the moss climbing the cracks,
the rich dark pelt of the moss;
I see that not everything is wrecked,
expectation never ends,
I can't quite believe it,
but then I can't not believe it.

THE NEWS IN TRANSLATION

Even while death falls on us
we can't keep our faces straight
but break up, laughter bursts out.
The rhetoric of pain requires
in those who feel it
the perception of an audience,
actors and their audiences.

But there in the empty bedroom
when the audience is gone at last
and you cannot hear yourself
and the script blurs and the sweat
dries in the dark, purpose disappears
and you laugh because the audience has turned away
bored, weary, satiated, spiteful
you have turned away.

Your double existence, along with the conviction
of its importance, maintains
a solemn belief in messages.
What is death saying? What is pain saying?
You hope that the inflections,
the loud and soft, the rise and fall will carry
enough information to keep both of you busy.
And to keep both listening.

But though you struggle painfully to feel it,
alone you can't feel pain for long—
your arm burns in a dream, the acid wound
parts in a dream. Only a yawning breathlessness remains
as a symbol of your vigil.
You throw open the window
to inhale the night air, to gasp,
then to laugh silently,
and the dark outlines of the buildings

trace your eyes from corner to corner.
You tell yourself that you can't stand it.
How does that sound? "I can't stand it!
I can't stand it!"

THE GREENHOUSE EFFECT REACHES THE ENVIRONMENTAL AGENCY

A personal, small alarm
goes off in his heart,
and then his eyes pop open.
What is the future eating?
He hears only loud and soft,
the rise and fall of words
outside the room.

Alone, he can't feel for long—
is that how a real drought feels?
He doesn't know what he has done
does the sky want to die?—
The smell of the street entering
mingles with the burning Amazon.

He throws his window wide
to inhale the night, to gasp,
to force his old bureaucratic smile,
and trace the dark buildings'
muffled edges with his eyes.
There is an orange glow from the East,
a mantle over the earth.
He used to talk about the ozone layer,
and paper would float across his desk.
Biodegradable.

In the night "Biodegradable"
has the ponderous foot of a dinosaur.
But the glowing air throws back the word,
and there's an odor of warm smoke
twenty years from now.

THE QUAKE

Slammed to the earth
and knowing how light he was
when he reached for the patio post
and it moved, knowing
not only that he had fallen
but that his children, his wife,
had been thrown somewhere
and it had nothing to do with him,
his skin tight on his face
as if scorched all day by the sun,
out of control; out of control, he saw
the apricot tree swirl
as it whipped the fence.

Oh boy! This was bad, this was
blindside, and would it stop?
The phrasing of the patio slats
was wrong, and the steps of ascent
and descent, the nature of ambition
cracked. If the last was first
and the patio warm on his back,
then would he rise with new eyes?
He had not said goodbye to anything.
His bones were shifting
in their meaning, and the power lines
danced over the yard,
over the sound of doors
or walls opening and slamming.

He sat up like a convalescent
and watched the pots swing
in their macramé nets,
saw the light brighter
than before, and the brown paint
of his hand stippled with pebbles

flooding with red. Then stood
in the middle of the yard
calling out "Honey! Honey!"
as if he had discovered
the huge rock of the earth.

OLD MRS. GILBERT'S HOUSE AT FOX HOLLOW
"I will arise and go now. . ."
—W.B. Yeats

I will return to you and away from the news,
to the pebbles at the edge of a clear stream
and the summer house over the stream
where you keep butter and milk, headache
cold soda in bottles hung in the water
in midday when bees drone out of holes
in the mud, when the live oak simmers
and spider webs kneel in the crofts of branches.
Eternity and completion in the quick water
and the slippery bottom. There the sky
and complex dreams land on grass blades
and blur there drying and pulsing. There
you come with school teacher frowns to heal
us, to sooth twitching legs in cool water,
to gently pull down, with hard hands,
the future, to pull up the past where I
yawn and dream, and forget anger.
Childhood is a warm stone in my chest,
where I am vulnerable to the air,
where my eyes burn with sweat.
I am prepared to go, I packed my heart
and locked the fifty questions in my desk.
I will stay there working for you until night.

FOR K.

The power lines slanting over my porch
call on your blood as current from Prague,
and against your suffering you have made a bed
of little houses. You were never
necessary, and therein lay your beauty.
Terrible accidents cover the valley, they are
strewn about like honey cakes your mother
made you eat. There is no end to healing,
and the sun comes up on your dark face

still pointed over tiresome ledgers.
You construct the corridors
and empty chairs with leather arms,
and questions that smell of mildewed wool.
You are not the need but the great surprise
of darkness, your ink-stained fingers
in the shadows of the maple leaves,
your eyelids the grey sheath on the redwood.
You help starlings tumble from the sky.

You never praised things as they are.
You had foreseen the death camps in trees,
you do the constant work of senselessness.
Because of you, the sunlight and I
are crazy on the porch while delicate
trains cross the valley, coming and going,
white worms on the black edge of justice.
The world carved out of light
for crowds of onlookers and a yawning panther.

ARBOR

It would have protected me,
arching over for a long life.
The pine is painted rusty red
and makes a garden curve
over and above to hold and turn
what the sky shoots down. There was
the red, the grain, stapled,
and flaked edges of wood chewed out.
It is there to filter rain gently.

It is there to sit quietly
among trumpet vines and roses,
and all the spirits crowding
in hope it will create in peace
a haven where one by one we could
pass through up the hill
into herb smelling air,
to see the city prickling the sky
across the bay, defiant, against
heaven. It was our hope,
for the earth has no arbor.

We could say there's an arch
over us, green air for dancing,
for bringing shovels and wheelbarrows,
for sheer whistling as the sow bugs roll,
as the flea bane sets out small petals.
The redwood arbor is fragile,
made by our hands, staggering under roses.
We dreamed it was our mothers looming,
their curved arms comforting
when the sun blares down.
It is rainbow and moon, eclipse, straddle.

All of us born without flak jackets,

without stingers, all of us loam
among rocks, among bees tumbling flowers.
Because nothing was there
we built wooden arches—they are caves,
nest, defiance, they make air sweeter
and we breathe for a moment.
We decided to take our stand in the garden
until staggering wood falls
and heavy stems lay on the ground.
But we can't stay, the skydoor is thrown open,
and we go out into rubble.

THE HAWK

Yesterday when I was tired
I looked outside and saw that eyelash
spiraling down between me and the tree,
then behind the tree.
It was a desperate filament—
so few mice around in the poisoned valley—
but it moved easily.
It was not the kind of bullet bird
that cuts the day in half.
This one was black against the fog
and nothing against the tree,
and height dropped from it like shavings.
Some birds are made of sound,
some of emotion like the hundred names
of distance. This one was made of praise,
this one kept envy under its nails,
the hate that trills and thumps
and tries to look like Spanish tile.
Sinking, the hawk had nothing more to want
than its own hunger.
Some things can just tilt and fall,
and in their ease create their grace.
I could not hear the air
become a comb for its wings,
yet it turned and bore the weight
of my eyes and tin can childhood. Then
it was gone hunting somewhere,
and the scrolling name it left,
slanted across my window, did not appear
except as vacant signature.

BECAUSE YOU TOOK THREE SPOONS OF SUGAR

Suddenly I saw you. Three spoons!
How could I forget?
One emotion I can understand
that comes to me clearly, is recognition.
The crust of habit fell away
and our lives grew comprehensible
the way the soles of shoes create a dark bloom
after months of walking and standing,
and the soft glint of scarred leather is recognizable.
But now that you saw me, your eyes sharpened.

> A cockroach pulses under the shelf
> when the moon surveys the kitchen
> and marks it for appetite

as if to deny me, as if ancient desires only
were allowed whereas utensils, sweeteners, fabric, hands,
were not only distractions but insults.
I confess that you didn't exist until I saw
what you did with the sugar. In memory I can't even hear
you talking. How did I answer any of your questions?
I recognized you as if you were my own hand
turning lavender at the fingertips.
That is, I saw you even though
what you thought was yours I created for you
and was created for me, and you
held the spoon down the way I do when you stirred.
And if not you, then I don't know.
Can I see you? Or who?

MY HOPI BUCKLE

The silver sweats to silver,
the black base works
to give up its secrets.
The humpbacked flutist
calling for my wife,
calling the water,
the buckle dances on my belt.
This buckle is the plate
in my daughter's head,
this buckle is my shoe.
This buckle fashions
the forgetting years.

The three flutists crippled
as I am, give their lungs
to the bellows, they bow
before the bench pin.
They lie on the bench pin
waiting for the awl, they kneel
before the flat mill file.
The desert circles them,
the leather hammers,
the long-nosed pliers.
Smooth to my hand,
burnishing my hand,
the wave pattern
saws into the desert.

SPACING

This is the house, this is the street,
everybody's house, nobody's street.
I know there is not enough room,
and I'm afraid for my daughters.

They grow thin and more people
fill the space they surrender.
The leaves of the walnut in the rain
twitch like the innocent

in the ethnic wars.
Why should there be everyone?
All down the street people are at dinner
while it rains. Are they laughing?

We will be roaming the streets with guns.
What is this vertigo
when you don't know who you are?
You could be one like the rain.

The time has come to double the planet,
this will give us a few years
to give to our daughters
beside streams, for them to sit

on the clean squealing grass.
We can do it if we all blow
deeply into the earth. There will be
more space for farms, more land,

though we can't hope to understand.
With more space the dinners will improve.
There will be rich desserts,
and a spoon to hold tight

until the pattern of the handle
burns into your finger and thumb,
and you are printed, like everyone, forever.
Then the anonymous rain will sweep

down the street, black, shining,
blustering but only seeming to be angry,
and begin its search for pale roots,
each separate tendril, growing,

searching the space while there is time.

THE UTILITY MAN

I can't convince myself that cleaning
the alley is spiritual discipline,
only I've got to clear the way
to the yard for the man from

Water and Power to read the meters.
The endless wall and the leaves pointing
down carry the light, sound comes to me
through the haze of sun as if my childhood

lay along my bones listening for a call.
And daylight ticks in the pigskin paint
of the house as I pant among splinters
and lint stuck to lengths of wood,

trying to collect myself because I don't
know what to do with all the junk. My
God! I don't have to know, sweat
has a way of happening anyway, and a new

arrangement of the shells of things,
the wire frames of tomato plants we won't
plant, with spiked ends to press down
somewhere into the ground of being.

HE HAS WON A PRIZE

First he walked up and down,
then he sat in his chair and stood up.
Now he could breathe the chemical air.

He opened the door to the playhouse—
the bitter damp came out to dance
around him in his bunny suit
with the future on his forehead.
Many things that once were wrong
were right. He would open stupid books
without a flare of hate
as if they had been childhood friends.
He threw a punch at the air.
He could renegotiate his contract
with the fig tree and the birch
whose sore eyes never healed.
He was worth more now.

The future and the past
now stood around the yard like waiters.
A noontime of awards
reserved a patio chair
and a long lime drink of minutes.
This was the hour to kick back,
to give the suffering earth and suffering ants
some free time.

THE JUDGMENT

I walked home from the meeting
bruised, having hurt myself
saying inane things and lying,
and there was the tree quiet
overhead, with great ridged bark
I could put my fingers into.
Maybe my skin was that thick
to someone who had walked across
my way. Flowers, crisp and
dead, lined the driveway,
and I knew that what was allotted
to my middle-class life
could only be taken seriously
by people like me.

The cat was waiting without accusation
at the window, and he rubbed
against the glass when he saw me;
it was clear that the evening, at least,
had no unusual expectations.
I felt I could say anything
into the twilight puddled on the doorstep.
The origin of twilight in the turning
earth, relaxed on the doorstep.
I could, if I wanted to,
say nothing to the front door,
and yet the door would open.

Then the cat was rubbing my ankles,
and when I looked back before going in
and saw the dark leaves unmoving
against the slightly lighter sky,
and there was no wind driving the moon,
I hurried to go inside.
Then when I had entered the house

I glanced with shame at the pictures which pointed me out. I had chosen those pictures and they had chosen me, unlike the others, the leaves.

ACQUITTING THE LOOTERS

They conspire in quiet with nothing to do,
all the people slow breathing
who would grow strong in others and so move
out to the street. The piles of glass grit
on the walks tell them what to do.
They know each other with a flick of eyes.
They meet themselves in and out of broken doors
with their hope and, finding slavery,
carry winged shoes and VCR's
like poultices under shirts,
under arms against their aching sides.

With every stroke the beaten take control,
carry white blurring into darkness.
It is power, the way of understanding
where you are. The one with stolen underwear,
with the case of beer, with the three bikes,
the lights come on in his skin
and he knows his friends. They sat
starving among objects waiting to return
to the place they dreamed of. Now, beautiful
the handlebars, gleam of deprivation.
This time they ride the city
and their spokes flash.

MY FATE: UNOCAL

In the corner of my eye I see a gas station attendant
when I drive by at night, and the rain-slick station
glows with insignia, the man in the jump-suit
lounging against a smooth white wall. I can see
suddenly his blackened hands, his corrugated nails,
my hands, my nails. When I stop to talk
with Ernie or go to George McLain, I don't confess
my fear of being them, holding a grease rag,
punching in the numbers, connecting with the big
oil company that drains their blood and drags it
to the orange ball mooning over the station.
Through nightmare I understand what happens here.
The man with the car phone in the BMW,
a huge insect, holds out a credit card
without a look at me, my distant smile.
My cap can't hide my obsequious ears.
I know I wear a name-tag on my chest,
beneath the skin, and my feet encase thick shoes.
I write my license number on a slip, snap
the paper quickly, and step back from myself.
Forgive me, George, because I don't want to be you,
or to look into your heavy eyes, my eyes.
I don't want to breathe exhaust, steaming,
rising white and red, delicious.
It's not enough for me to gaze under the hood
watching myself pour a pink liquid jewel
into a well, or to lean over girls,
dark under their eyes, perfume from their windows.
I am surly, I always want my shift to be done,
when I can peel envelopes from my skin
and drink to confidence at the Twilight Bar.
But when the ball, spinning slowly, glints,
and gas fumes rev up my lungs until I'm dizzy,
when the moon hangs, smoking, above the sign,
I know I'm there, with you, pumping gas, full serve.

FRACTALS

Since I was ten I knew there was a continent
with a fragmented coast where I must live
but which my eyes, it didn't matter where I
looked, pushed away.
Now when I hold the charts of chaos,
Mandelbrot sets, my hand trembles.
There is my continent, the exploded lines
and untouched colors I had begun to think
couldn't exist. Its face scattered brown and green
crazy with roots
like a tuft of grass upturned. The muddy rivers
rich with flies under the trees
go nowhere understandable, not
to the ocean through cane brake
and cattails, not to any lake
composed against an empty sky like right and wrong.
Everything is unlike everything,
my first sunrise.

I can't say what happened in the years
until now. If I say Denver or San Francisco
I begin to laugh. If I say I helped someone
tremendous silence follows.

Now I see the fractured place where I belong.
Let's say I am alone there,
there is no pattern even a god could find.
And my uneven house with a few absurd dishes,
let's say, is unrecognizable to anyone
but me. Whoever wishes
can go there, it has no borders, it's free.
These are the portraits I suspected
when I was ten,
the freedom I could share,
insane with oxygen.

DOGS WELCOME

I reach for the leash, ready for a walk.
He is rising out of himself to gallop on the ceiling.
He touches me with guilt. Am I responsible, being human,
for this delight? As I expected,
he stops and writhes, tongue out
and sliding between black prim lips like silk lining.
He will make a fool of everyone today,
sit up, give paw, call himself retriever,
golden self poised for something better,
tapping nails on the tile floor, collapsing
to lay his nose to a shoe. Unfulfilled,
he sniffs everyday at his bowl and the cupboard door,
daylight empty in his eyes, hope in his sprung hindlegs,

but now he flares up as we rush down the driveway.
He is so ordinary he would disappear
without the orange lantern of his body in the sun.
His mission is to smell the day.
His growling lurks so deeply he doesn't know it,
stiffens his ears briefly then drops away. He abandons
himself to my tugs on the choke chain
as he lightly guides his white chin, his ecru rump ruff,
his placid skull smooth as a seal skin.
Every aspect of his skin at one with every other,
trotting his immortality and forgiveness.
Crazy for strangers, crazy for bones, crazy for us,
he once bit through a fence that kept him from home.

I trudge beside him past the cat that stares
from the open window sill at Paula's house,
but he won't fake a move, and the cat won't move.
Whatever in him once pledged to love or die, snarling,
all nose and canines in golden fields, now
lies quiet riding like a baby in his chest.
The street rises before us, there's a broken pavement,

a new roof, a dog banging at my neighbor's gate.
I hold on as we walk, purposeful not going anywhere.
We pull each other on the same round journey.

THE PHONE RINGS

1.

My communiques never catch up with her
and now if she ever stops
they will drown her
pouring from city to city.
I have made a fictional daughter from memory
with a lot of eye shadow
but the outline of her weakens
as if it had been scraped from the inside
until ready to collapse.
My language grows more foreign.
What she is doing I am doing.
Ah, if I could convince myself
then I might convince her
that what is out of reach
will reach toward me,
I am water for blind roots
that feel for water.
I am the water that longs
for stubborn tendrils.

2.

Her news is familiar
like recognition in the mirror
of a stranger. The passage
of surprise to the languor of memory
is so fast it can't speak before it
turns away, becomes wordless
again and again, all the same.
Of course we talk by phone
but she doesn't come through,
some imposter twists a voice
and pushes it toward me.

Her freedom has amazing space
peopled by kids with towering hair
on corners in Greenwich Village.
I pull space out of myself I cannot cross.
Instead I become a housekey,
a windshield, a father.
And will always give this to her.

WELTERWEIGHT
BARNEY ROSS

1.

In the fourth round stone legs
in the fifth round Hammering Henry
in the sixth round inquisitors came
to shake their keys in his eyes
in the seventh round wired to the canvas
in the eighth the dance was done
and his breath froze and broke upon his mouth
in the tenth he would not fall
in the eleventh he could not stand or fall
in the fifteenth forgot the web of blood
the scraps and locker rooms
heavy bag light bag rights and bolos
caught in his sharp spine bones
when Henry Armstrong forked his body

But his arms remained he threw
the classic hook when he was gone
"Hebrew-American" with eyebrows grown together
from Chicago with sleep round head
his knotted legs screwed down
in May of the 1938 Hitler year
above cigarettes and fedoras
in a dome of punches over the crowd
his losses and wins dropped away
from his horse-power shoulders
and his ribs like iron rails
they carried the heart that brought him

In the last round's glistening
he was finished and would not go down
Barnet Rosofsky caught cornered
heart's petals eased under ringlights
he showed no mercy in New York
to anyone who loved him
just to stand and keep standing

his slitted swollen eyes stinging
he could go on losing
he lost but he would not fall
he could not forgive them his courage
he walked from the ring into his past

2. May 30 1934

If courage is not the will to die
why did he step through the dark

through the craft in his shoulders
into the square of light

like the highlight in a dead eye
why did he whip clubbed hands at McLarnin

"Baby Face" the Irish darling
a good man with a right

he sold us he grabbed Jimmy
for Mama the kids the "pals"

who hung upon his arms
heavy above the ringside dogs

he was raised above faces
from the shadows of their losses

his muscles yearned for Jimmy's
face in the other corner

then they began the dance around
each other's fire Jew and Irishman

Jew Jew Kike Sheeny Jewboy Jew
and Jimmy the black Irish paddy

each a "credit to his race"
over the fierce stare of cigars

McLarnin sweet on the gloves
bursting through his jaw

to the long grey line of depression
to faces drawn back from shadow

to coins of light and bells
ringing his immortality

caught in the cameras' flashes
raising his arms in pure loved light

stunned free and healing
riding with Mama in an open car

3.

And those he fought
Tony Canzoneri Sammy Fuller Billy Petrolle
Pete Nebo Frankie Klick
Kid Morro Bobby Pacho
Jimmy McLarnin

Jimmy McLarnin
Bobby Pacho Frankie Klick Henry Woods
Jimmy McLarnin

Young men with flower buds between their legs
and their flesh the air around a tree

Baby Joe Gans Ceferino Garcia
Ceferino Garcia
Lou Halper Gordon Wallace
Chuck Woods Laddie Tonelli Morrie Sherman
the long line of suffering bodies
victims of their strength
with broken hands

Phil Furr Izzy Janazzo
Al Manfredo Chuck Woods Jackie Burke
Al Manfredo
Ceferino Garcia

Henry Schaft Bobby Venner
Henry Armstrong
will not lie down
stand quietly in the dark uncounted
the blood dry on their mouthpieces

4.

Abraham Washington "The Little Hebrew" Attell Benny Leonard Al Fields were among fists fought after Black Aby Gideon the Jew Ikey Pig Ugly Baruch Levy the Yokel Jew Barnet Barney Rosofsky from Chicago and bagels on Maxwell Street and the smoke was full of garlic and people then years and the bout for fifteen rounds in the interests of charity age 24 weight 137 ushers guides and special police Fight Site Accessible by Subway and Elevated Lines and the odds 6 to 5 take your pick change for the Flushing train to Bliss Street burning pace and blinding attack with 7 prelims

Blackbeard Jack Dempsey refereed and among the spectators laughed Postmaster General Farley and Mayor LeGuardia A G Vanderbilt Walter Annenberg James Fitzsimmons Willie Saunders the jockey who rode Omaha to victory in the Derby and Preakness into the darkness out of the newspapers when Ross beat Canzoneri when Ross beat Petrolle when Ross beat McLarnin when Ross threw grenades when Ross posed with Father Gehring on Guadalcanal when Ross took the morphine stairs after the War and his legs in spasms when he kicked the habit and walked out of Lexington to Cathy again

But "many in throng voiced disapproval" of the decision over Jimmy the upper and lower grandstands disagreed Pop Foster disagreed McLarnin disagreed the opening four-rounder went to Ralph Vona of Asbury Park Al Jolson Joe Penner Irving Berlin Victor Moore Fannie Brice shined in attendance "he got cut in the lip in the first" McLarnin led with a light left to the face and Ross stepped in and clipped the welter champion with two hard lefts to the jaw it was blood they shared in the spring night for the first time in his long career and although the straw hat season was two weeks old topcoats were still in evidence and eyesockets hollowed by light and hummingbirds waiting to hover

5.

At the ends of my wrists
I have a place of wins and losses
when I jump into the canvas

warm under my towel
with whatever I have done
out of my will and moves

I won't go down I speak
the language of how I live
mama watch me take him

where are the movie stars?
O my friends you will love
my heart become his heart

do you love me?
I'll eat his fucking heart
and his hope will fail

I fight for the Milk Fund
and I feed regret
for the living drop by drop

for a moment you see clearly
the mouthpiece flying
and my cut eye's bright blood

6. Guadalcanal 1942

>"This is me with my pal Father Gehring
>and parrots on our shoulders"

They forgot themselves on an island
the war was not a war
the country was not their country
everything they knew had feathers
and talked from their shoulders
"I laid on my back
and threw grenades over my head"

They could win Silver Stars
they could forgive America
the pain of their fathers
the shrapnel could visit them
in their arms and shoulders
and whisper to their brothers
how the dream of fighting
was simple in the green land

They had broad cardboard leaves
and shining grass to look at
jungle rot malarial shakes
the palm trees that ached for life
in that nightmare their rifles'
needles stitched up the night

Greasy bullets followed them
their sleep could offer hope to anyone
they told their stories his hands shook
pulling the unraveled laces of his gloves
"It wasn't like the fight game"
whoever they fought they fought again
then they were hungry
and their grenades bit the earth

They went to long hospitals and fever
to pick the delicate threads of morphine
wrapped around their spines

7.

> "The ear can detect a whole apocalypse
> in the starry night of the human body"
> —Jean Cocteau

I left the beloved world
                      and when convulsions hit
            I began to bounce on the bed
I want to tell you how it was
      so you know me vomiting every cell
      Cathy Cathy I moan
                      eating my city of friends
and my knuckles the foothills carved by the sun
because you left me in Lexington
                      always kicking the habit
there was your outline
                      and it was gone
I held the string of my pajamas
trying to make you again to form you
      but my hands jumped
the little table hated me it told me to forget
      it wanted me naked
it wanted me to sweat pounding the floor
stomped by dead marines in boxing gloves
      and the guys from the press saying
                  Barney didn't make it
and you would disappear

in the room my wooden skin tracked by memory
I threw my shoes at the mirror
                to kick the mirror
I contracted into a needle
I looked through a pinhole and there was the world
      and you on the other side looking for me
            to lie down with you again
free in the honey corners of your mouth

my honored grateful skin transparent
                      convinced of you

I wanted you to know me in the grey room
                      in the fluttering rain of ashes
begging the dark voice of my father
to deny for me that I was there
                      in my cell gristle and bone
how I was nothing how I had no courage
and sat hopeless in my chair
and never deserved to look at you
    how I wanted morphine more than you
I wanted you to know
                      nothing stops the collaboration of iron
                      nothing would stop your eyes

8.

Barney Ross
you were my sleep with scarred eyes
dark against the light
your black hair gleamed like a fender
your broken nose
your humbled ears
your eyebrows of blackbirds
punished for flying

I was written by you
with nothing but your courage

Barney Ross
your breathing was hitting
you shuffled and slipped punches
you danced a way of being
across the ring wrapped in rope and darkness
spit in a bucket
the quiet marrow blind in your bones
your heart without alternatives
telling stories of what wins and losses

You were the arms of silence
behind voices

Barney Ross
caught up in ringlights
standing in your shoes and trunks alone
with your kidney punch
and your hook and clinch
when you stopped and drew a shuddering breath
then hugged the decade
that held you in its arms

Your last fight the giving and rescue

your art in blood.

OTHER WRITINGS

TO THOSE WHO WILL READ ME

Ah, you want me to tell you things like 'I-was-born-in-El-Biar-in-the-suburbs-of-Algiers-in-a-petit-bourgeois-Jewish-family which-was-assimilated-but...' Is this really necessary? I just couldn't do it, you'll have to help me...

—Jacques Derrida

It has not always been this way, but we have arrived at a condition in which ethnicity is disappearing because of its very presence. To be a Jewish writer or a Chicano, Native-American, African-American, or Asian-American writer has become less marginalized, less distinct, because we have become more and more a country, even a world, aware of difference, discrimination and oppression. In spite of backlash, the spirit of diversity continues to capture the world. There is no generally "American" writer, no "Great American Novel" and there never will be; we are all regionalists, we all have an ethnicity out of which we write, whether we disguise it or not, or even when we do not perceive that it exists. I write as a Jew and this singles me out just as Faulkner is singled out as a Southern writer. At one time we amused ourselves by believing that Iowans or Ohioans were "American," forgetting that their ethnicity was real though ill-defined because of an American fantasy that there was an essential America. Even if we were a people united, and that is doubtful, we are not one people.

We are composed of groups, races, ethnicities, regions, clubs. There are groups everywhere of all varieties, some of them more distinct or important than others. Belonging to a square-dancing club is arguably less important than being an African American or the member of a religious community. But we are in the process of acknowledging and accepting a wide range of beliefs, conditions, communities, identities. We are beginning to understand that we cannot lump all Asians under one designation, that there are significant differences between Japanese, Chinese, Koreans, Filipinos, Cambodians, Malaysians, Taiwanese, and so on. My mother, who came from Odessa, spoke of Galitzianers and Hungarishe with contempt, and I heard from her how members of one shtetl cursed the members of another shtetl. But that was in an age when differences were somehow wrong, when there was a great and, as it proved, destructive urgency toward unity. It was an age when the quest for unity was often a mask for the quest for power. The Soviet Union opposition. We have begun to understand that to be different is not necessarily to be bad, and that though we may not like our neighbors we have an obligation to tolerate them. We may even debate and discuss our differences. Only in the light of tolerance and freedom can the discovery of what we share be a celebration.

I support the right of any person to address the members of his group. But in order for a writer to write specifically and only for his group he must adopt a code understood only by his group; and even that code can be broken and its meaning flood into general understanding, as the code of Black Gospel singing broke, as the "rap" code is breaking into the awareness of a popular audience. We have reached a point where ethnicity cannot be coded for long, nor can regionalisms, nationalisms, nor even those arts which speak to different religions. We demand to hear and to be heard, we want justice.

I feel at home in this environment. I also acknowledge that as a poet I must speak to a small audience—I imagine there are more bowlers than people who read poetry. Yet even this audience reaches beyond ethnicity. Charles Reznikoff was a Jewish writer, Gerald Stern and Philip Levine are Jewish writers, but their audience, of course, is not confined to Jews. In my poems I do not address Jews only, but I write out of an experience colored by my identifications with the place of my birth, Pittsburgh, with my immigrant father and mother, with the Yiddish I heard as a child and would not speak, with my reading of Dostoyevsky, Tolstoy, Flaubert, I.B. Singer, Garcia Marquez, Mandelstam, Rilke, Garcia Lorca, Tillie Olsen, Yeats and Whitman and Dickinson, Yehuda Amichai, Ginsberg, Richard Wright and James Wright. I write out of who I am colored by, from which I am not distinct. I have written a sequence based on Buddhist statuary, and other poems which no ethnic "tags" appear as signs to know, and I certainly don't want to infuse my work with a self-consciously Jewish sensibility or language. I think most of us would agree that *Death of a Salesman* is Jewish in its way, though ethnic signals do not appear obviously in that work. The "Jewish" we must have is insight and difference.

We need room, we push against the boundaries of prejudice, we want to move, punish, and appear to each other. I want to celebrate experience, but I view celebration as a serious matter, as a victory after long defeats, as an entry into the deepest reality which I take to be consonant with the finest imagination. I see metaphor as a glorious act of tolerance. If I fall short, and I do, I have learned to go on anyway toward celebration.

Such celebration would be like finding justice at last, temporarily perceived, soon dissolving. Not justice as compensation to me for wrongs done, but justice which includes me in its balance, which gives equal weight to all of being, and to rescue those others who believe they have no ethnicity, that they are somehow mankind and are therefore right. Our job is to relieve them of their vagueness and to entice them to join us in that job and to enter, insofar as words can enter, into the discovery and delineation of what matters.

Certainly I identify with Israel, with the Holocaust, with my childhood when my little gentile friends told me I had killed Jesus. And I both seriously and not so seriously await the knock on the door which tells me to get out. Such aspects of myself are not to be discounted, just as my differences from my friend John Hartzog are not discounted; and yet I believe that to dwell on my differences with others is to share our differences, and my friend Ricardo Means-Ybarra as a Chicano writer addresses everybody. Should all streets, all gardens, all houses be the same? I speak to those who will listen, and if they see themselves in me, it will be through our difference. I have never written a poem which was not Jewish, or American, or myself.

A few words on my long poem about the great modernist Russian poet, "Mandelstam." Aside from well-known figures and places evident in the text, Alexey Nikolayevich Tolstoy was a member of the great Tolstoy family, but not a direct descendent of Leo. A nobleman, a count, he sided with the Whites and went into exile to escape the Bolsheviks. Later, he worked himself back into their favor, was allowed to return to Russia in 1922, and became a notable and serviceable Soviet novelist. Cherdyn was Mandelstam's first place of exile before he was allowed to choose Voronezh. Here he tried to commit suicide by jumping from a window. Kolyma was the prison camp where Mandelstam is said to have died in 1938, either of heart problems, as the Soviets claimed, or by being frozen to death. Princess Salomeya was the beautiful woman to whom Mandelstam wrote the poem, "Solominka," in 1916. Savinkov was a terrorist and later Minister of War under Kerensky. Yagoda was the head of the Cheka, the Soviet Secret Police, later purged by Stalin.

Benjamin Saltman

March 31, 1993

Dear Nick—

I may not have told you that Ricardo and I and some other poets were invited to an Academy Awards party at a plush restaurant in Century City called Tripps. Suzanne Lummis was the one who supplied the names to the organizer of the party, someone named Michael Bass, who routinely gives parties and who has some interest in promoting poetry. He is organizing a huge amateur poetry festival in Los Angeles in July. Anyway, Ricardo and I received a letter from Anthony Quinn (!) inviting us to this black tie affair, and for the hell of it, and in my case, to give Marjorie a kick, we went. It was very strange, a party for old-timers in film and tv, as well as wanna-bes, open bar, buffet dinner. The poets' contribution was to read short poems during the commercials while the Academy Awards presentations were going on! On closed-circuit tv, at the party, and thank God neither Ricardo nor I were asked to perform. Wanda Coleman read, Austin Strauss read, and other LA people I didn't recognize. Diane Ladd read a poem from *Look Homeward Angel*, but was very bad tempered because people were not listening. Virginia Mayo (!) introduced a young woman poet friend from Australia. It was a strange, cluttered, gate-crashed, food-run-out, on-the-make, bimbo girls in $3000 dresses affair. I had two bloody mary's and a glass of champagne, but Ricardo and Cynthia got drunk. Marjorie filled up on Coca-Cola, and Helen was at CSUN teaching a night class. Cameras everywhere, dress slipping down off the breasts of the young ladies. A strange conglomeration of people, Gary Coleman, Dick Van Patten, Maximillian Schell, Peggy

Lee, Herve Villachaiz ("De plane! De plane!") Weird Al Yankovic, Mickey Dolenz, William Windom, McDonald Cary, etc. People looked at you as if they expected you to recognize them. I met a young woman from Croatia who said she loved the poetry of Sergei Esenin—what a shock. She knew about Mayakovsky as well.

I've sent some queries about jobs in the Bay Area, and sent out some poems to magazines. Tonight I begin teaching a creative writing workshop for senior citizens at a senior center here in the valley. I'm excited about it, about the challenge. Basically, I am spending my time writing and preparing to write. I would also like to do some more reviews.

Enclosed are a few recent poems you haven't seen, and as usual I hope you have time to comment on them. The poem about the bears is strangely on the subject you brought up in your letter—about the limitations of language. I certainly don't agree with the usual sense of Rumi's epigram quotes by Michael Hannon, but I believe both he and Hannon have an idea that many poets have had, especially the religious ones. The notion appears most prominently in mystical writing, in which the mystic claims that the union with God is beyond description, beyond words, and that only in symbols and parallels can the poet deal with the divine. Dante reached the end of the Divine Comedy when he beheld God surrounded by angels looking like a huge multi-foliate rose (the angels ranged around like rose petals around their center) and then wrote, "and I could speak no more." This is known as the "ineffable" nature of religious experience, and I think Hannon is quite religious and is involved with that mystical silence in which God exists and which the poem can only leave space for. It's in that context that language fails precisely because it posits a condition beyond language. But traditionally there is another convention adopted by poets and lyricists, the artistic scam, wherein the poet who claims that words cannot capture the beauty of the beloved proceeds to write elaborately about her anyway! It's a kind of false modesty, in which the poet hopes that his words will be dazzling anyway. It is in this last tradition that my somewhat ironic "Alaskan Special" is written. In dealing with the difficulty of trying to envision the marvelous bears, which have come to me through television, I playfully capture (I hope) in language something of their strangeness and magnificence. Thus the paradox of the successful failure. The poem itself is a celebration of empathy through language and differs radically from a poem like Galway Kinnell's "The Bear" which I feel is hokum—the poet kills the bear, enters the bear, and becomes the bear.

I agree with your attitude about words, as well. Although I call poetry the "dirty art" because words are so deeply connected to our fallen selves, our guilts and values, I think it is precisely because of its engaging so much of our inner lives and our minds that it is also our greatest art.

Take care of yourself, my friend.

Ben

AN ALASKAN SPECIAL
    "I'll sing and whistle romping with the bears."
                           —Theodore Roethke

Watching the brown bear lying on her back
nursing two huge balls of fur, I think
of the craft and love it would take to see them
again in words. How I am constricted
by the screen that constricts her life
triggered by seasons and the sockeye salmon.
I see her wet body as she fishes
and how strong she is, muscled verbs along
her driven back. I must believe since I have nothing else
to fashion my belief. Words conform her rank smell,
her lathered mouth, her nipples of black sucked
rubber among ambiguous flowers. She reclines
nuzzled in the sun open as language anyone can use.
There is promise in her blood pushed back on the hill,
her cubs lurch toward her open breast.
are these vowels the open sounds of her
mysterious life? The mountains sustain her,
each berry and tuft of fur torn from her passing,
from birth to death to birth thrust amid lupine.

Was it a blessing that she could not look at me?
She must return to the stream to claw, blooding
the shining salmon. How could she ask for tawny
words to illuminate summer and affirm her time?
The contentment of mating on the warm hillside
prophecy the rending and devouring of her dead cub.
Words dissolve on her wide-open eyes.

The shadow of a lens rides the complicated earth
like water, and if I were that shadow
I could ride her and sooth the spiny hair
around her sour muzzle. But it is the bear that hovers

and makes the grass, no less than television phosphor,
coalesce. Not me. Now when her great head
imprints on me, now in her roaring breath, I'm caught;
I'm called to yield the swaying land,
draw stiff brush and rocks around me, and offer solace
to anyone who, like me, sprawls among burrs and pebbles
and echoing words. When she runs across the field,
the ripple of her fur lifts a river to the sun.

When the wildflowers went tumbling down
to the rocky waters, I began to see, as if caught
in a kaleidoscope, these acts stumping
among rocks. And I wondered if the gravel substrate
on which the scene depended collapsed in consonants,
whether the words of my own distress collapsed too
amid roiling water and gray rocks, the talking,
lush water, the mother's milk. I could not doubt
that all had come together, that the bears would drag
out with huge digging claws all the earth they needed
to make a place for sleep,
so they might grow silent.
Or that, shoulder to shoulder, clawing for salmon
in a brotherhood of feasting, they would celebrate.
When they looked up from raking the season,
would they see the green turn silver?

At times, tortured by light, they might call
the cranberries, the blueberries, and wild sedge
so that we might see each other and settle differences.
The news is waiting, the raking of a claw across an arm
would invade an indifferent room. Amid the confused
cries of all who want to live, she waddles over rocks,
back along her path, then drops down to shoulder
over her toed-in paws crowded by her cubs.
The berries ripen and the summer shakes. She moves,
seductive in the lurch of time, in the language of her longing,
the autumn cloud bringing the first snow.

PHOTO BY ELLIOTT ERWITT

COUGHING WITH BERT

I don't know exactly how or when I met Bert Meyers. In my first semester he was just there, living with his wife and two kids in Claremont not far from the college. At first I lived across the freeway from Claremont in Montclair, then I moved to El Monte and drove once or twice a week to Hollywood to the Vedanta Temple to hear Swami Prabhavananda or to celebrate a holiday such as the birthday of Sri Ramakrishna. The swami remained important to me, and certainly I pursued my studies with intensity, but Bert was a poet, and it seemed I had been looking for him all my life. I saw in him the kind of drive I had when I was writing stories but which now, after the pressures of a job, a bad marriage, a transformed religious life, and a sense of failure, I had virtually abandoned. Bert was my age, he had persisted, he had published a number of poems, and had just published a book with Swallow Press called *Early Rain*. Numerous poets knew him and admired him, poets I had read and who were writing well, Robert Bly, Louis Simpson, William Pillin.

In Bert's narrow handsome face and sad smile I saw my own intense belief. His melancholy images placed him among writers who have been forced into dreaming by the narrow path of their lives. He had spent some years as a gilder for a picture framing company; he glued extraordinarily thin layers of gold onto frames. He was a workman and in fact had never gone to college, but was allowed into the master's program at Claremont Graduate School on the strength of his poetry and the recommendations of the friends he had made among scholars and poets. The Claremont English Department was willing to take a chance on a man who had not taken English in college and had never written reports or term papers. They had also taken a chance on me—my flights into community college teaching, my years with a nutty school like Emerson. I was the son of a peddler, Bert was a craftsman; we understood each other's ambition, we shared a suspicion of the middle class. We both felt that somehow we had slipped into the class-conscious environment of Claremont past a cordon of scholars who would probably kick us out if they only knew what we thought of scholarship. Like me Bert was here because he might land a job out of it, but poetry was on his mind as Vedanta was on mine. I respected Bert's belief in poetry. He was enthralled by words. He loved to intone his poems: "Stars climb girders of light. . . ." Complex as a man and poet, he proclaimed himself to be simple. He identified with self-taught poets like William Blake and John Clare, and disliked the esoteric intellectualism of T.S. Eliot and Ezra Pound. I can see his thick curly hair, his broad wrinkled forehead, the strong bones over his eyes, and his sly contempt when he mentioned Eliot and Pound. After a seminar at school I would go to his house and sit in his front room over coffee, and he would try out a poem, a line, a word, and look for my reaction. I was impressed by his confidence in me—I had gotten used to the arrogance of writers who held their opinions to be sacred and their work untouchable. But Bert worried an image like a dog a bone, tearing at it, trying to crack it. If it couldn't sustain his criticism, he would dispose of it.

"What about a sea gull, the sound it makes," he said." You know, the cry of a sea gull, it's like the squeal of an iron gate."

"That . . . sharp cry. Yes."
"What if I called it a gate opening in the sky?"
"All right, I guess. What's the poem about?"
"Things I've seen."
"I like it."
"Do you?"

So we would talk about lines and images, about whether they were accurate or false. I started to write a few lines, short poems; I had written poetry sporadically and without satisfaction ever since I started writing. When I arrived Bert's wife would greet me with a sweet smile and return to the back of the house to attend her son Danny. I loved Bert's metaphors; he reminded me of Keats and Dickinson and a poet I had just begun to read, Rilke. I understood Bert because, like me, he was fascinated by strange connections between language and reality. To him imagination was not just making things up; it was the truth which appeared pulsing as if alive between language and reality.

> The towns were tables, set
> by the road each night.

You had to see what Bert was saying, see how at night on a flat road like a table, the towns were glasses and plates and silverware rising and gleaming in the moonlight—with light shining from the windows. He loved the miracle of metaphor, and his narrow face hovered over the paper tablet in which he scrawled his lines. I could see what he saw. And when he wrote,

> At the end of the day
> I drive home
> the proud cattle of my hands,

I saw his knuckles like the rump bones of cattle rising from the steering wheel of his car after a day's work. His hands worked for him, he was a craftsman, and he captured this labor and his joy.

No wonder I would visit almost every day after school. Here we were, two men in their thirties, with some fairly desperate experience behind us, laboring over words. All that had happened to me had remained dammed up, it had not found sufficient place in my stories. Now I saw how through images I could at least begin to release it. I had an instinctive love of words, metaphors; I heard the sounds of words in my mind even when I read silently, I made their cadence and associations mine. "They've eaten buttered stone," I wrote:

> "Every glass is dead,
> soldiers cross the world with a plan,
> they've died before, they'll die again."

My days of staring at my typewriter, of walking at night now focused on poems. I could *feel* that I was capturing whatever reality I knew. I was still meditating every day, I was writing paper after paper in graduate school, but my heart expanded; this was what I could give, these lines I made not just for myself but for anyone who cared. "Children tumble from the veins and roll away, tiny cars." I cared about the way mechanisms captured us. Bert also cared in his melancholy, sometimes bitter way. In his days working as a gilder he had stolen books he loved because he could not afford them, he stuck them in his big overcoat. He had a bookshelf of poets, many I had not heard of: Attila Jozsef, Miklos Radnoti, Antonio Machado, Georg Trackl. Marvelous poets even in translation from the Europe I identified with. One thing had kept me from writing poetry was that my contemporaries in American and English poetry seemed over-crafted, too interested in word play and formal cleverness. John Crowe Ransom was affectedly witty, Richard Wilbur was hollow, Robert Lowell lacked an ear for cadence and sound. On the other hand, I had just begun to read Louis Simpson and James Wright, writers I could take to my heart; they sensed tragic undertones in American society, repression and exploitation glossed over with glibness. Bert introduced me to other Americans who diverged from the mainstream, Robert Francis and William Stafford, for example. We barely mourned the death of John F.

Kennedy, the American who loved to flex his muscles. The excitement ran high. The protests begun by the Beats were merging with the civil rights and anti-war movements; a more open poetry was being written under the influence of writers from continental Europe. Although I was prepared to study Eliot and Pound and Yeats in graduate school, I could not admire them as persons, their snobbery, their fascist tendencies; they acted as if they owned the English language which because of my ethnicity and class I was forbidden to use. Bert Meyers felt this oppression as much as I did. I was attached to Vedanta but could never forget that I was a Jew, that my father had been a peddler, that I had been enticed by my society to hate myself.

> beginning because the day begins,
> because dreams like sick bees stumble from my eyes,
> because a man has more than hands
> and hates the ignorance of his room,
> I waken and will eat!

My poems appeared to be lyrics, personal songs, but beneath that surface I was protesting my (man's) cultural and even cosmic imprisonment. I remembered the white crust of dirt on the legs of black kids I played with. I saw the Navy nurse look at me with contempt. I saw my mother's stockings twisted on her thin calves. It was in images that the complexity of the world came to me; at least so it seemed. At last I had a friend who agreed with me and who could see the things I saw. When I wrote about cars on the freeway: "Our earth rocks its children/in curved glass," I knew Bert would understand the curve of the windshield, our isolation behind glass, our almost helpless infancy "rocked" by the earth; and he would even sense the underlying implications of the lines: rocks thrown against glass. There would be no escape. Like me, Bert loved images that burst into meaning, that carried the content which other writers tried to express discursively. As I wrote more I realized that I wanted to write poems always risking rejection, poems which would not rely on obvious rhymes or patterns but on the living cadences of an inner voice. I was ready now to turn away from the techniques which made poems "attractive" but which in reality cut readers off from inner experience. I clung to statements like Williams' "No ideas but in things" and Creeley's "Form is nothing more or less than an extension of content." But these were not creeds; Williams and Creeley helped me keep faith in what I wanted to do: to write poems which grew without obstruction and began at the center of my consciousness. Out of my memories of lying in bed in a long hospital ward, out of my sense of the pathetic sacrifices of the young in war, out of the twisting and turning of my religious blundering, I could imagine wounded soldiers in a field looking up at trees:

> Dazed above their heads,
> the leaves are chrome: society.
>
> Then between the apples and the apples
> they see home,
> the blue trees of their homeland.

Though these lines are from an early poem, "Blue with Blue," they carry theories which have persisted, which I never abandoned once I started writing with Bert Meyers. The look of chrome is the blinding glint of leaves in the sun; and that is translated into "society," something hard, impenetrable. And the apples in the poem are what we want from society (with an obvious reference to the fruit of the Tree of Knowledge), but in the spaces between apples and apples and leaves and leaves one sees the sky which in a kind of blinding reverse image is itself a tree, the "blue trees" of our ultimate "homeland." The poem contains the notions of being, of God, which developed from my practice and study of Vedanta; it also echoes my hospital experiences. I am not concerned whether my poems are good or bad, but with how they struck at what I believed. Often the images of my poems are "absolute"; they arise from my self almost without justification. Often I commit myself to a poem in spite of the risk of not being understood. I am willing not to understand everything in another's poems—the poems of Celan and Mandelstam and Vallejo fascinate me in their absoluteness. Even if I did not fully understand the reverse image of the blue trees in the poem above, the relationship between cosmic and cultural experience. I was prepared even before I met Bert to enter into such mysteries. I had been fascinated by surrealism at San Francisco State and surrealistic influences of poets like Ginsberg and Gerard Malanga. So when I met Bert everything in my past as a writer and reader came together, and Bert was there to welcome me.

He could expect me to understand what he was doing and even to help him decide on revisions to his poems-in-progress. We read books of poetry as they came out, we discussed our course work, we went to bookstores, and later we took a trip to Santa Barbara to hear Thich Nhat Hanh, the Vietnamese monk and poet. I was upset that there were not enough people able to appreciate Bert's keen vision or the accuracy of his melancholy sense of America. Even when his second book, *The Dark Birds*, was published in 1968 by Doubleday, he did not reach the New

York establishment, would not pull the strings which might get him readings in New York or on the college circuit.

It is Bert's eyes that I remember, his voice like a cello when he read his poems. He was strong when I first met him, and he still liked to chin himself from the branch of a tree in his yard. In high school he had been a rope climber, but later he ruined his health smoking. When I met him, he had the beginnings of emphysema but could not stop smoking, though he tried various kinds of exotic filters and long brown cigarettes which were supposed to be low in tar. Cigarettes and coffee, a note pad, a table and lamp—he needed ritual objects to bring him into a poem. I never discussed it with him, and watched him get worse, until he would break into a terrible rattling cough—which chilled me reminding me of my stay on the tuberculosis ward. Bert's sickness merged with his poetry and became one with it; his sad poems then rose up with the fate of Jews in this century:

> The dark birds came,
> I didn't know their name.
>
> They walked in Hebrew on the sand
> so I'd understand.

Bird tracks on the sand look like Hebrew letters and, typical of Bert's rich vision, spoke of the impermanence of their lives and of the terrible anonymity of the Jews who perished in the Holocaust. His French-born wife had been hidden by Catholics during the war, and he clearly dissociated himself from the Los Angeles and American materialism, as if he had become a citizen of a strange country composed of the political left, European poetry,

Israel, and imagination. I know from conversation with others that Bert seemed exotic to others, visionary on the one hand and childishly simple on the other. That wasn't the Bert I knew, a deeply committed poet who was, among other things, competitive, angry, mockingly brilliant, playful. It was easy for me to identify with him and yet, finally, to be puzzled by his depressions, his arrogance. I chose to know the Bert who saw the coming of winter in his "October Poem":

> When I came home, after work,
> I saw an old man mow his lawn.
> Sweet rain fell from those blades, and death
> smelled like a baby in its bed.

Many who read this poem would fail to see the winter in it or smell and sense the rich implications of the mowed grass as in Frost's poem "Mowing." I can picture now Bert's face of winter, his thick gray hair, the deep lines in his forehead and around his mouth. It seems that John Keats and Dylan Thomas and Sylvia Plath died too soon. But what can we really say about early death? All lives have a curve defined by their end or not defined at all. Bert died in his early fifties, but the shape of his unlived life goes on meandering along a shore, in lamp light in a quiet room, in the smell of grass.

Photograph by Helen Saltman. Copyright © 1993.

BIOGRAPHICAL NOTE

Benjamin Saltman was born in Pittsburgh, Pennsylvania, in 1927. He began writing poetry seriously in 1965. *Blue With Blue*, his first book of poems, published by Lillabulero Press, appeared in 1968. Since then he published seven other books: *The Leaves The People*, Red Hill Press, 1977; *Elegies Of Place*, Armchair Press, 1977; *Deck*, Ithaca House, 1979; *Five Poems*, Santa Susana Press, 1989; *The Book Of Moss*, 1992, Garden Street Press; *The Sun Takes Us Away: New And Selected Poems*, Red Hen Press, 1996; and *Sleep And Death The Dream*, published posthumously by Red Hen Press, 1999; and the 2017 re-edition of his *Book of Moss*. This marks his eleventh book of verse. During his life, he received many awards including two NEA Fellowships; a Chester H. Jones Foundation Award; and an Anna Rosenberg Award for a poem about the Jewish experience. His work has appeared in numerous magazines and periodicals, among them *Poetry Northwest, Southern Poetry Review, The Hudson Review, Mississippi Review, The North American Review, The Iowa Review, Shirim, Poetry/LA, Bakunin, Asylum Press,* and *Kayak,* to name a few.

From 1967 to 1992, he taught verse writing and contemporary American literature at California State University, Northridge and was a visiting professor of English at Bowling Green State University, in Ohio. During his years teaching at CSUN, he lived with his wife, Helen, and three daughters, Jeanmarie, Lara, and Majorie, in Northridge, California and later, after retirement, he lived in Kensington, California near Berkeley, until his death in 1999. He also completed a memoir titled, *A Termite Memoir*, about his life writing poetry and his many relationships and marriage to his wife, Helen. He once wrote, "What you need to know about me you can find in my poems."

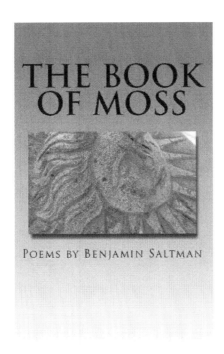

Image of cover of *The Book of Moss*. Copyright © 2016 by Garden Street Press.

Praise for *The Book of Moss*:

"These poems are wonderfully restless, always in a hurry. Benjamin Saltman can make waxing the car or just sitting in a 'cool place' a sort of sports event for the mind. Yet the poems close firmly, some about the Poet Self, some with humor and sadness about Us. Here are the lonely but warm observations of an exceptional talent: a fine collection."

Reed Whittemore

"Benjamin Saltman is among the most graceful and gentle poets living in Los Angeles or anywhere. I'm very glad to see this collection which contains many poems I've admired for years and new prizes as well."

James Krusoe, *Santa Monica Review*

"Everyone who knows Ben Saltman comments on his rare and humble sensibility; indeed, this is the quality that leaps off the page. Saltman notices details as if he had been gone for a long time and returned to a strange sad planet that he still loves. There is something else to love and that is [Saltman's] stately acceptance of the passage of time, as he 'lengthen(s) toward sleep.' In the first poem of the collection, 'Myself As A House,' Saltman writes, 'Please convince me that holding on/is as good as flying,' and after you close the book it seems as though Saltman has done both."

Susan Salter Reynolds, *Los Angeles Times*, August 30th, 1993, Review of the First Edition of *The Book of Moss*

SAN LUIS OBISPO, CALIFORNIA

For further information about this book and poet, Benjamin Saltman, one may write to editor at the address below:

Nicholas Campbell

5969 Entrada Avenue

Box 9

Atascadero, CA 93422

USA

Made in the USA
Columbia, SC
02 April 2018